Welcome to a treasure trove of strength and inspiration. This book of affirmations is a whispered guide, offering unwavering support to every woman in the transformative journey of motherhood.

Each affirmation is a beacon of resilience and hope, embracing the unique power found within the challenges and beauty of matrescence. Join us in discovering these affirmations, crafted to empower and uplift through every step of this extraordinary path.

Introduction

Welcome, dear mothers, to a journey of transformation, growth, and self-discovery — a journey also called matrescence. This book is an embracing hand, a warm hug, and a guiding light through the beautiful and often challenging path of motherhood.

In these pages, you'll find a treasury of affirmations — words crafted with care and understanding, tailored specifically for the incredible women undergoing the wondrous transition into motherhood. Matrescence is not merely a phase; it's a journey that marks the beginning of an enduring, beautiful story— a story of strength, resilience, and boundless love.

This book is here to remind you that amidst the whirlwind of change, you are not alone. Together, let us explore the diverse landscape of emotions, the intricacies of transformation, and the unspoken truths of this remarkable journey.

From the moment you felt the flutter of anticipation, to the overwhelming joy at the first cry of your child, you've been embarking on an

3

expedition — full of moments that inspire, challenge, and shape you into the incredible woman you are becoming.

Through each passage, each sentiment, and each whisper of affirmation, our goal is to uplift you, encourage you, and celebrate the depth of your experience as a mother. You are the heartbeat of your family, the source of endless love, and a beacon of strength and guidance.

This book is an ode to your courage, your spirit, and your unwavering love. It's a reminder that in every step, every tear, every smile, and every milestone, you are writing a story that is uniquely yours.

So, settle in, find comfort in these words, and allow them to be a companion through the moments of uncertainty and the milestones of joy. This journey of matrescence is about you, your strength, your vulnerabilities, and the beautiful metamorphosis you're undergoing.

From one mother to another, know that you are extraordinary, cherished, and appreciated. You are enough. You are loved. You are where you need to be.

So what is Matrescence?

Matrescence is the physical, emotional, hormonal and social transition to becoming a mother.

Understanding the Journey of Motherhood.

Matrescence, a term coined by anthropologist Dana Raphael and later introduced into psychology by clinical psychologist Aurelie Athan, encapsulates the transformative process women undergo as they transition into motherhood. It defines the multifaceted changes — physical, emotional, psychological, and social — that women experience during this pivotal phase, akin to the metamorphosis of a butterfly.

Understanding matrescence offers a new lens through which to comprehend the journey of motherhood. Much like adolescence prepares individuals for adulthood, matrescence prepares women for the significant role of motherhood. This awareness allows us to acknowledge the intricate and complex changes a woman undergoes, acknowledging that becoming a mother is not merely a biological shift but a profound transformation encompassing various dimensions of her being.

This recognition of matrescence can reshape how we embrace motherhood and view mothers within our society. It invites a more empathetic and supportive approach, fostering understanding and

alidation of the challenges faced by women in
his transitional period. Ultimately, embracing
matrescence leads to a shift in societal
ttitudes, offering a platform that encourages
pen conversations and a supportive
nvironment for mothers to navigate this
ransformative phase.

he impact of acknowledging matrescence
oes beyond individual experiences; it sets the
tage for a more inclusive and supportive
ociety — one that values and respects the
iverse and profound journey of motherhood.

It's time to begin your journey with these affirmations.

My hope is that each heartfelt whisper brings you both joy and strength.

I am transforming into a stronger version of myself through motherhood.

1. I am transforming into a stronger version of myself through motherhood:

Motherhood is a transformative journey that strengthens your resilience, patience, and adaptability. Each day, you become a more formidable and empowered version of yourself, ready to embrace new challenges.

Every day, I embrace the beauty of change within me.

. Every day, I embrace the beauty of change within me:

Change is a constant in motherhood, and every day brings new experiences. Embrace these changes as the threads that weave the beautiful tapestry of your journey.

I trust my instincts
as I navigate the
journey of motherhood.

3. I trust my instincts as I navigate the journey of motherhood:

Trust your inner wisdom and intuition. Your instincts are a valuable compass as you navigate the twists and turns of motherhood, helping you make the best decisions for your child.

My love and strength grow with each step of this transformative path.

4. My love and strength grow with each step of this transformative path:

With each step on your motherhood journey, your love and strength grow. The challenges you face are opportunities for your love to expand, and your strength to deepen

I am worthy of self-care and nurturing during this time.

. I am worthy of self-care and nurturing
during this time:

You are worthy of self-care and nurturing.
Taking care of yourself ensures that you have
the energy and resilience to provide the best
care for your child. It's not selfish; it's essential.

I am becoming a beacon of love and guidance for my child.

6. I am becoming a beacon of love and guidance for my child:

Your role as a mother is to be a guiding light, providing love, support, and guidance for your child. You shine brightly in your child's world, helping them find their way.

*I release any fear
and embrace the joy
of this new chapter.*

7. I release any fear and embrace the joy of this new chapter:

Let go of fear and embrace the joy of this new chapter in your life. Motherhood is a journey filled with love and happiness, and it's okay to fully embrace it.

*My body is a vessel
of creation and resilience.*

. My body is a vessel of creation and resilience:

our body has carried and nurtured life. It's a
essel of creation and a symbol of resilience.
mbrace and honor the strength and beauty of
our body.

*I am adaptable
and capable of handling
the challenges that
come my way.*

9. I am adaptable and capable of handling the challenges that come my way:

Motherhood presents various challenges, but you are adaptable and capable. You have the strength to navigate these challenges and find solutions with grace.

I am an empowered mother, ready to face whatever comes my way.

10. I am an empowered mother, ready to face whatever comes my way:

You are an empowered mother, equipped to face whatever comes your way. Trust in your abilities, your love, and your resilience.

I am patient with myself as I adjust to the changes within and around me.

1. I am patient with myself as I adjust to the changes within and around me:

Be patient with yourself as you adjust to the changes of motherhood. It's a process, and it's okay to take your time to adapt and find your balance.

My journey through matrescence is unique and beautiful.

12. My journey through matrescence is unique and beautiful:

Your journey through matrescence is unlike anyone else's. It's unique and beautiful, with its own ups and downs, twists and turns, and moments of sheer beauty.

*I trust the timing of
my transformation into
motherhood.*

13. I trust the timing of my transformation into motherhood:

Trust that your transformation into motherhood is happening at the right time for you. Your journey is unfolding as it should, and each step is a part of your unique story.

I am learning and growing through each experience on this path.

4. I am learning and growing through each experience on this path:

Each experience in motherhood is a chance for learning and growth. Embrace these moments of discovery and see them as opportunities for personal development.

*I am surrounded
by a community of mothers
who support and uplift me.*

15. I am surrounded by a community of mothers who support and uplift me:

Recognize that you are not alone on this journey. You have a supportive community of mothers who understand and uplift you in times of need.

I am embracing the unknown with an open heart and mind.

16. I am embracing the unknown with an open heart and mind:

The unknown can be both exciting and challenging. Embrace it with an open heart and mind, as it's where you'll find new adventures and discoveries.

I am creating a safe and loving environment for my child to thrive.

7. I am creating a safe and loving environment for my child to thrive:

Your role as a mother is to create a safe and loving environment where your child can flourish and grow. It's a gift you provide every day.

I am finding strength in vulnerability as I navigate this journey.

18. I am finding strength in vulnerability as I navigate this journey:

Vulnerability is not a weakness; it's a source of strength. As you navigate motherhood, being open and vulnerable allows you to connect more deeply with yourself and others.

I am capable of handling both the highs and lows of motherhood.

19. I am capable of handling both the highs and lows of motherhood:

Motherhood is a journey with highs and lows. You are capable of handling both with grace, finding strength in adversity and joy in the wonderful moments.

*I am grateful for
the lessons and growth
that matrescence brings.*

0. I am grateful for the lessons and growth that matrescence brings:

Matrescence is a period of growth and transformation. Be grateful for the lessons it offers and the personal growth it inspires.

I am finding balance between caring for myself and caring for my child.

21. I am finding balance between caring for myself and caring for my child:

Balancing self-care and child care is essential for your well-being and your child's. Finding this balance is an ongoing process, and it's a testament to your dedication.

*I am patient with
my progress and trust the
process of transformation.*

22. I am patient with my progress and trust the process of transformation:

Be patient with your progress through transformation. Trust the process and the timing, knowing that each step is leading you to where you need to be.

I am radiating love, joy, and positivity as I embrace motherhood.

3. I am radiating love, joy, and positivity as I embrace motherhood:

Radiate love, joy, and positivity as you embrace motherhood. These qualities will enrich your own experience and the lives of those around you.

*I am honouring my
emotions and allowing
them to guide me.*

24. I am honouring my emotions and allowing them to guide me:

Honour your emotions and allow them to be your guides. Your feelings are valid, and they can lead you toward self-discovery and understanding.

*I am a vessel of
unconditional love
for my child.*

25. I am a vessel of unconditional love for my child:

Your love for your child is unconditional and boundless. You are a vessel of this incredible love, nurturing your child's growth and happiness.

I am resilient and capable of adapting to new roles and responsibilities.

6. I am resilient and capable of adapting to new roles and responsibilities:

You are resilient and capable of adapting to new roles and responsibilities. Motherhood brings change, and you have the strength to embrace it.

I am connected to
the rhythm of life as
I embrace this journey.

27. I am connected to the rhythm of life as I embrace this journey:

Motherhood connects you to the natural rhythm of life. Embrace this connection and find harmony in the cyclical nature of your journey.

I am open to receiving support and guidance from those around me.

28. I am open to receiving support and guidance from those around me:

Be open to receiving support and guidance from others. You don't have to navigate this journey alone; there are people who are willing to help and uplift you.

*I am celebrating
every milestone and
moment of this journey.*

9. I am celebrating every milestone and moment of this journey:

Celebrate every milestone, no matter how small, and cherish each moment of your journey. These moments are what make your path as a mother extraordinary.

I am nurturing my inner strength and wisdom as a mother.

30. I am nurturing my inner strength and wisdom as a mother:

As a mother, you're not only nurturing your child but also your inner strength and wisdom. Trust in your intuition and the valuable wisdom you gain through experience.

*I am creating a bond
of love and trust with
my child.*

31. I am creating a bond of love and trust with my child:

Every day, you're creating a bond of love and trust with your child. This bond is a powerful source of security and love in their life.

I am proud of the woman I am becoming through motherhood.

52. I am proud of the woman I am becoming through motherhood:

Be proud of the woman you are becoming through motherhood. You are evolving, growing, and discovering the incredible strength within you.

I am confident in my ability to make choices that benefit my family.

33. I am confident in my ability to make choices that benefit my family:

Have confidence in your ability to make choices that benefit your family. Your decisions are made with love and care for their well-being.

I am embracing the beauty of both my strengths and vulnerabilities.

34. I am embracing the beauty of both my strengths and vulnerabilities:

Embrace both your strengths and vulnerabilities. They are part of what makes you uniquely beautiful and powerful as a mother.

*I am finding peace
and harmony in
the midst of change.*

5. I am finding peace and harmony in the midst of change:

Find peace and harmony within yourself, even in the midst of change. This inner tranquillity will help you navigate the shifts and transformations of motherhood.

I am gracefully letting go of what no longer serves me on this journey.

36. I am gracefully letting go of what no longer serves me on this journey:

Gracefully let go of what no longer serves you on this journey. Release the past to make space for new experiences and personal growth.

*I am a vessel of life,
carrying both love and
wisdom for my child.*

37. I am a vessel of life, carrying both love and wisdom for my child:

You are a vessel of life, carrying not only love but also wisdom for your child. Share these gifts to shape their world and their future.

I am patient with myself as I adjust to the new rhythms of life.

8. I am patient with myself as I adjust to the new rhythms of life:

Be patient with yourself as you adjust to the new rhythms of life in motherhood. These changes take time, and it's okay to navigate them at your own pace.

*I am embracing
the present moment
and finding joy in it.*

39. I am embracing the present moment and finding joy in it:

Embrace the present moment and find joy in it. The small, everyday moments are often the most beautiful and meaningful.

I am discovering my own unique way of being a mother.

40. I am discovering my own unique way of being a mother:

You are discovering your own unique way of being a mother. Your journey is personal and one-of-a-kind, shaped by your experiences and your love.

I am open to receiving the blessings and lessons of motherhood.

1. I am open to receiving the blessings and lessons of motherhood:

Be open to receiving both the blessings and lessons of motherhood. Each experience, whether joyful or challenging, offers valuable insights.

I am creating a legacy of love and strength for future generations.

42. I am creating a legacy of love and strength for future generations:

In your journey through motherhood, you are creating a legacy of love and strength that will resonate with future generations. Your love and wisdom will leave a lasting impact.

I am honouring my needs and practicing self-compassion.

43. I am honouring my needs and practicing self-compassion:

Honour your needs and practice self-compassion. Taking care of yourself is an act of love, and it ensures that you have the energy to care for your family.

I am finding beauty in the challenges and growth in the moments of ease.

4. I am finding beauty in the challenges and growth in the moments of ease:

both challenges and moments of ease, you can find beauty and growth. These experiences contribute to the depth and richness of your journey.

I am a source of comfort, love, and security for my child.

45. I am a source of comfort, love, and security for my child:

You are a source of comfort, love, and security for your child. Your presence provides a safe haven where they can thrive.

I am allowing myself
to bloom and flourish
on this journey.

46. I am allowing myself to bloom and flourish on this journey:

Allow yourself to bloom and flourish on this journey. Like a flower, you are constantly growing and revealing your unique beauty.

I am resilient and capable of handling whatever comes my way.

47. I am resilient and capable of handling whatever comes my way:

You are resilient and capable of handling whatever comes your way. Trust in your strength to overcome challenges and embrace joy.

I am embracing
the full spectrum of
emotions as a mother.

48. I am embracing the full spectrum of emotions as a mother:

Embrace the full spectrum of emotions as a mother. Your emotions are a rich tapestry, and experiencing them fully is a testament to your authenticity and depth.

I am connecting with the wisdom of generations before me.

49. I am connecting with the wisdom of generations before me:

Your journey as a mother connects you with the wisdom of generations before you. Learn from this wisdom and let it guide you.

I am nurturing the bond between my heart and my child's heart.

50. I am nurturing the bond between my heart and my child's heart:

Every day, you nurture the bond between your heart and your child's heart. This deep connection is a source of love and strength.

I am grateful for
the gift of motherhood
and the lessons it brings.

51. I am grateful for the gift of motherhood and the lessons it brings:

Be grateful for the gift of motherhood and the valuable lessons it brings. Each day is a precious opportunity to learn, grow, and love.

I am a strong, loving, and empowered mother, and I am exactly where I need to be.

52. I am a strong, loving, and empowered mother, and I am exactly where I need to be:

You are a strong, loving, and empowered mother, and you are exactly where you need to be on your journey. Trust in yourself and the path you are walking.

Conclusion: Embracing Matrescence

Throughout this book, we've embarked on an intense journey — a journey that speaks to the heart of every mother traversing the path of matrescence. These affirmations, carefully crafted and thoughtfully shared, are more than just words on a page. They're echoes of your story, reflections of your resilience, and affirmations of your incredible strength.

As you reach the end of these affirmations, remember that each sentiment, each whisper of encouragement, is a beacon of light in your journey. Motherhood isn't just a destination; it's an ongoing voyage that unfolds in beautiful and challenging ways.

The experiences shared in these pages are not just anecdotes; they are a collective embrace — a nod to the shared emotions, fears, hopes, and triumphs that bind mothers together. As you reflect on the sentiments expressed here, may you find solace, reassurance, and a gentle push forward.

every challenge, in every tear, and in every laughter, you're evolving into a remarkable woman — a woman who cherishes her past, embraces her present, and looks forward to her future.

Motherhood, with its complexities and wonders, a testament to your adaptability, resilience, and unwavering love. Your journey through matrescence is a canvas, painted with moments that transcend the mundane and define the extraordinary.

May these affirmations serve as a reminder of your incredible capabilities, your undying love, and the unique strengths that shape you into an exceptional mother. You are writing a story — a legacy — filled with love, wisdom, and immeasurable courage.

So, as you close this chapter, remember: you are more than enough, you are loved beyond measure, and you are exactly where you need to be.

With love and solidarity,

Amanda Murray

Printed in Great Britain
by Amazon